Biographies of famous people to support
the National Curriculum.

Alexander Graham Bell

by Emma Fischel

Illustrations by Lesley Bisseker

FRANKLIN WATTS

LONDON • NEW YORK • SYDNEY

First published in 1996
This edition 1998

Franklin Watts
96 Leonard Street
London
EC2A 4RH

Franklin Watts Australia
14 Mars Road
Lane Cove
NSW 2066

ISBN: 0 7496 2419 1

A CIP catalogue record for this book
is available from the British Library.

Dewey Decimal Classification Number: 621.386

10 9 8 7 6 5 4 3 2 1

Series editor: Sarah Ridley
Designer: Kirstie Billingham
Consultants: David Wray and Dr Anne Millard

Printed in Great Britain

Alexander Graham Bell

"It's a beautiful baby boy!" said the doctor.

His parents named him Alexander, just like his father and his father's father.

"Quick! Tell everyone the news!" said Alexander's father.

But the only way to tell the news was very slowly.

Most letters went by train, but even trains were slow.

There were no cars, and no phones either ...

... until, that is, the baby boy grew up and invented one.

Alexander was always inventing.
He invented a longer name
for himself.

"Alexander Bell is too short!" he
said.

He invented a special way of sending messages, too.

Alexander grew up in Edinburgh, Scotland, with his two brothers, Melville and Edward.

His mother was deaf and his father wasn't.

But his father WAS strict.

Alexander's grandfather was a teacher. So was Alexander's father.

"Now you are sixteen, Alexander, what do you want to be?" he asked.

"Errrm, a teacher?" said Alexander.

Alexander's father taught people
who found it hard to speak.
Some stammered or stuttered
but most of them were deaf.

Alexander taught in lots of schools. He made his lessons fun.

Like his father, he helped deaf children feel and see how sounds were made. It made it easier for them to learn to speak.

13

Then something very sad happened. When Alexander was twenty-three, his brothers died of an illness called tuberculosis.

Today there are medicines that could make them better. But there weren't then.

"We'll move to Canada,"
Alexander's father said.
"Lots of fresh air will stop
you getting ill."

It took many weeks to get
to Canada.

Back in Scotland, Alexander and his father had done some special drawings to help deaf people. The pictures helped them make the right shape with their mouth when they spoke a word.

People in Canada thought the
drawings were very clever. One
person thought they were very,
VERY clever. She asked
Alexander to come and teach
at her school in America.

Soon important people in American heard about Alexander.

He was made a professor at Boston University.

He also began to teach a girl called Mabel Hubbard to speak. Mabel was fifteen and she had been deaf since she was four.

Alexander was twenty-six by this time. Mabel didn't like him much to start with but later she changed her mind.

A new way of sending messages had just started up. It was called a telegram.

Messages were sent down wires in a code of dots and dashes. The trouble was, a long message ...

... meant a long queue.

Alexander thought there must be a way to speed it up.

Alexander taught all day, then worked most of the night on his new idea. He didn't have much sleep, or much money.

"I'll help you out," said Mabel's father. "You pay me back when your idea works."

Mabel's father was very rich. He hoped Alexander's idea would make him even richer.

Now Alexander could afford a work room. But he still needed one more thing – a helper. At last he found one.

The two of them worked all hours on Alexander's new machine.

Until, one day it got all jammed up.

"Hang on," said Thomas.
"I'll unjam it."

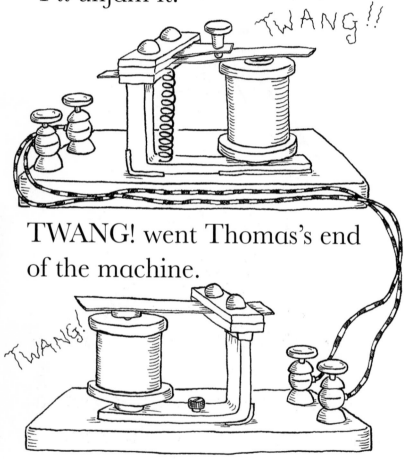

TWANG! went Thomas's end
of the machine.

TWANG! went Alexander's end
of the machine a moment later.

TWANG! went a brilliant idea
in Alexander's head.

That brilliant idea turned out to
be the telephone – in the end.

First there was a lot more work
to do.

Mabel's father was cross with Alexander.

"Stick to your idea for sending telegrams faster," he said. "Speaking down wires is a silly idea."

But not everyone thought it was. In fact someone in Chicago, called Elisha Gray, was working on just the same idea. And whoever got it working first stood to make a fortune.

So the race was on!

The trouble was, things kept going wrong.

At last they got it right.

31

But there was a big to-do.

Elisha Gray thought he had invented the idea. Alexander insisted that it was his idea first.

Important people looked through all their work. They soon decided.

"We declare, in this year of 1876, Alexander Graham Bell is the inventor of the telephone," they said.

Alexander showed his new
invention at a big exhibition
in Philadelphia.

The Emperor of Brazil tried it out.
"I hear, I hear!" yelled the
Emperor.

Alexander's telephone was a hit!

Although not everyone thought it was such a good idea at first.

The first phones were huge and difficult to use. Each phone could only ring one other phone.

Telephone wires cluttered up the street. Every telephone had its own wire. All the wires went above the ground.

But phones soon got better and
lots of people bought them.

That made Alexander rich, and
Mabel's father richer.

Alexander and Mabel married.
They went to Europe for their
honeymoon and received
an invitation.

Victoria Regina

from Queen Victoria
Buckingham Palace.

Dear Mr Bell,
    We are most interested in seeing
your clever new invention.
Please come to tea and bring it
    with you.

39

Alexander got medals and prizes for his new invention, and even more money. He gave lots of it away.

He set up a school for deaf children back in Scotland.

He built special places for
inventors to work in.

Alexander never stopped
thinking up new ideas.

Some flew.

Some floated, almost.

Some were soft and fluffy.

Alexander bought a house close to the sea in Canada. He spent a lot of time there with Mabel, his two children, Elsie and Marian, and, in time, with his grandchildren.

August 2nd 1922

He died there when he was 75.

Every single telephone in
Canada and America stopped
for one minute at the beginning
of his funeral.

Telephone Trivia

The Bell Telephone Company was established in 1877. It had a slow start as  only one hundred telephones were sold in the first year. After that it made lots of money for Alexander and his partners.

The first telephone exchange was set up in 1878 in Connecticut, USA. At last, a phone could speak to more than one other phone.

Alexander made the first wireless telephone in 1881. He showed it working between two boats about

three kilometres apart. But the idea
was not developed for years.

The first long distance call was between
Boston and New York, USA, in 1884.

The first transatlantic telephone link
was made five years after Alexander
died, in 1927.

Some important dates in Alexander Graham Bell's lifetime

1844   The first public telegraph system is set up in the USA to send telegrams.

1847   Alexander Graham Bell is born in Scotland.

1862   Alexander starts his working life as a teacher.

1870   The Bell family moves to Canada.

1871   Alexander moves to the USA to teach at the Boston School for Deaf Mutes.

1873   Alexander is made a professor at Boston University, USA.

1875   Alexander is working on the invention of the telephone.

1876   Alexander is officially said to be the inventor of the telephone.

1877   The Bell Telephone Company is set up.

1877   Alexander marries Mabel Hubbard.

1881   The first wireless telephone message is sent.

1887   Alexander improves the phonograph, which eventually becomes the record player.

1908   Alexander is working on the hydrofoil.

1922   Alexander dies, aged 75.